FRANK ORMSBY

THE Darkness
OF Snow

ERIC
BLOO
DAXE

BLOODAXE BOOKS

ISBN: 978 1 78037 366 9

First published 2017 by
Bloodaxe Books Ltd
Eastburn
South Park
Hexham
Northumberland NE46 1BS
UK

and by Wake Forest University Press in the USA.

www.bloodaxebooks.com
For further information about Bloodaxe titles
please visit our website or write to
the above address for a catalogue.

Supported using public funding by
**ARTS COUNCIL
ENGLAND**

Cover design: Neil Astley & Pamela Robertson-Pearce.

Printed in Great Britain by Bell & Bain Limited, Glasgow, Scotland, on
acid-free paper sourced from mills with FSC chain of custody certification.

For
Michael Longley
whose book this also is

ACKNOWLEDGEMENTS

Acknowledgements are due to the editors of the following publications in which some of these poems first appeared: *The Cincinnati Review*, *Devenish Townlands: Hectares of History and Heritage*, ed. Mary Maguire & Mary Doris (Devenish Heritage Association, 2016), *Hwaet! 20 Years of Ledbury Poetry Festival*, ed. Mark Fisher (Bloodaxe Books, 2016), *Irish Pages, New Hibernia Review, The New Yorker, Ploughshares, The Poetry Review, Poetry Ireland Review*, and *Salamander*.

The Parkinson's Poems was published as a pamphlet collection, *The Parkinson's Poems*, by Mariscat Press in 2016. I am indebted to Dr Kath MacDonald from the Division of Nursing, Queen Margaret University, Edinburgh who has used the Parkinson's poems as a teaching aid for both staff and students and has based a number of poetry session workshops on them.

A number of the poems have been broadcast on BBC Radio Ulster and BBC Northern Ireland.

CONTENTS

II

III TWENTY-SIX IRISH PAINTINGS

IV THE PARKINSON'S POEMS

V THE WILLOW FOREST

I

Where I grew up
the fields had names

Altar Boy

I cycle to town, rehearsing the Latin responses:
'Damn quell toffee cat, you've a tutta may.'
'Me a cowboy, me a cowboy, me a Mexican cowboy.'

I don my surplice and soutane,
ring the hand-bell and follow the priest
onto the altar. The congregation stand.

I am the half-priest, perfectly on cue
for the next forty minutes. Old Mrs Cassidy
tells me I'm a 'great cub'. I know this already.

Altar Boy Economics

A wedding paid better than a funeral.
We were tipped for smiling
and looking cute in photos.

Though sometimes a funeral paid better,
the mourners at a loss
and wanting to be thought generous.

Wedding tips could be displayed
with a discreet jingle, but funeral tips
were almost secrets, hoarded for rainy days.

A christening did not require an altar boy.
Christenings were, economically speaking,
a dead loss.

1959–1960

At twelve I am spilling poems
into tiny notebooks.
There is not a line
in the *Ambleside Book of Verse*
that I have not read.
I'm in a hurry all day, every day.
I can hardly keep up with myself
at study, at play. When I affect
a bookish silence
all winter under the Tilley,
my mother, too, is silent in her unease.

The Cash Railway

The annual bus trip to Enniskillen
to buy a school blazer
ends in Ferguson's, gents' outfitter,
with the little cable-car of cash
they call the Cash Railway
whirring up the wire
to the office on the first floor,
its companion descending
at the exact same speed.
At the point where the two cross
there is nothing in the world
that is off balance or out of sync.
You want to loiter there
for the next hour
and shout 'Bravo'
at every round
of funicular perfection.
But your mother is at the door,
lopsided with shopping,
reminding you that she has only two hands.

The National Anthem

Sinead feigned her fall.
A toffee girl, a gay run.
Binned. Arse. Loo.
Hard tune the hen-egg ruined.

Nil fuck-all Gaelige againn,
yet up we stand, the tricolour unfurls,
and we belt out the impassioned nonsense
we have learned by heart.

We think we know where we stand,
which side we'll be on
when the meaning becomes clear.

The Fields

Where I grew up
the fields had names,

The Brown Ground, The Brick-hole,
The Moss Bottom.

Earthed, each one,
in our practical affections.

Neddy

1

After much thought, the Cassidys
named their donkey 'Ned' or 'Neddy'.
He was grey all over, as donkeys ought to be
and had never, so far as was known, broken into a trot.
Too small to be called 'stately', he took the prize
for being patiently immobile. When we dressed him for work,
not a grey muscle moved until he was attired
in blinkers, hames and bellyband,
then reversed between the shafts of the cart.
This was when Neddy blossomed, like a grey rose.
If he had an ego it shone invisibly on the main road,
in the public eye, when a donkey could aspire
to cartwork of the highest order.

2

Released at the end of the day
into an empty field beside the farmhouse,
Neddy perfected the skills of idleness.
If you approached, he looked at you standing there
as though you were travelling too fast,
or were, somehow, in his unblinkered view, not grey enough.

3

Nobody told us immediately about Neddy's death,
or his burial in the woods. He made a slow
exit from our lives, being not-there daily
until we accepted that he would never return.
He was replaced by a grey tractor
that managed ten times his working speed
but didn't have a name.

Snow on the Way

The snow is in Olympian mode,
settling only on the mountains. Soon,
it will be cold enough for its residency
in the garden, its sorcery among the branches.

The Fox

Tree-silence, field-silence, snow-silence
welcome the fox to the edge of the plantation.
He is not surprised to see us
but nothing will break
that unblinking wariness. His narrow head
contains us, his eyes harbour the glint
of inhospitable winters. Nothing to be feared or gained,
he takes himself off, loping close to the hedge,
his hollow stomach gathering a fringe of snow.
We plunge and scatter home to announce the fox.
Will he be back tonight in search of our kitchen waste?
Is he cunning enough to avoid the gamekeeper's traps?
We'll stay awake, listening for his bark.

Owls

I am mesmerised by a gallery of roosting owls
in a child's compendium of birds.
Their eyes are ten floodlights in a wood.
You'd think their lives must be a *mardi gras*,
so richly feathered, so groomed to be at odds with darkness.
The invisible owls of boyhood, a secret of the groves,
come back to me, the mighty wingspan thrown, in my dreams,
across a tight clearing with no imagined escape.
Those claws disturb me still with their casual hint
of heraldic bloodshed. If these are wise owls,
what form does their wisdom take?
How did such handsome birds ever evolve
into nocturnal predators, their beaks turned down
to keep their victims in sight, their wings soundless?
Though they are thought of as ominous,
not everything in the lore of owls
is freighted with bad luck. Pliny the Elder records
that owls' eggs are a cure for hangovers...

Do You Renounce?

We stumbled early into the cold shower
of penitence and self-denial,
encouraged to think of life as a Vale of Tears
and ourselves as exiles.
Though deemed to have reached
the Age of Reason, we were too young to grasp
that the World, the Flesh and the Devil
were a lot to renounce
without a trial run. Nor did it occur
that what we had renounced that day
we might embrace fervently the next.
Through the red door to excess,
there was sport to be had,
or so it was whispered.
But we were crusaders then, zealously at war
with the monstrous trinity.
'Do you renounce?' roared the Bishop.
'Do you renounce?' roared the Priest.
'We do! We do! We do!'

Inoculation

The last polio child
in the parish
is dying indoors,
or parked on the front step
in a wheelchair.

Passing, we wave thoughtlessly
from the country of the immune,
those circles on our arms
– ring-forts, earthworks –
healing into the skin.

The Gang

At the Parish Carnival we are attracted first
to the sparky aggro of the bumping cars.
The jokes are all about fart-lighting and being
rammed up the arse. Really we are keeping an eye
on the tattooed specimen from Belfast who bounces
unerringly from car to car, untangling the knot
when all the girls drive into the same corner
at the same time. They shriek and do it again.
He frees them again. We fume and say nothing.
He is rumoured to be a boxer and we are afraid.
Barely deigning to take us
under his notice, he performs, again and again
the ballet of the bumping cars. We say 'Right! Right!'
and leave him to it and, with territory still to be won,
stop at the rifle-range and shoot dead
some wooden rabbits. At the ring-throwing stall,
somebody wins a doll and has to hide it
under his jacket as a present for his sister.
Well dare anyone challenge us now!
The town is ours, the night is ours, we lay claim to the stars.

Diversion

There are twelve signposts at the crossroads
on one vertical pole, the signpost tree.
Sometimes, for devilment, we turn the tree
half-circle, then settle to watch
strangers, sure of their destination, now doubly sure,
disappear trustingly down the road to nowhere
or the road to somewhere else.

Omagh

'You'll land me in Omagh,'
my mother groans,
at her wit's end.
Omagh is where the birdies are.
The out-of-mind drift
out of sight a while,
then back among us.
It is said that madness
runs in families.
We mooch around our gate
and think of it travelling at speed
in the shape of Miss Carty,
who, home again,
has joined the Dippers
and cycles the main road
in suspenders and knickers.

Rhododendrons

Or, as we said, 'rosydandrums',
never having seen the written word.
Privileged along the avenue to the castle
they trumpeted colour, were evergreen
and privileged again in the off seasons
when they held themselves in wait
for the next sumptuous budding.
Patrician growths. We had no urge to climb them
or hide under their skirts. What would we do
with such extravagance, such ostentatious flowering?
We planted five modest slips on the patch of grass
between the house and the main road.
If bushes could look embarrassed... We kept them there
as better than nothing to embellish the view.
Shabby in the sun, poor cousins in the rain,
they succumbed at last to the football we kicked among them
and the main road's dust, between showers, on their generous leaves.

Ruts

Cart-wide, tractor-wide,
the ruts spanning our lanes
were scored with an ugly beauty.
Whether they were a hard pattern underfoot
or whether we picked our steps
delicately between the lines,
they hold in the memory
as a carved track of our working days,
a rough signature. When the rain
turned them into watery trenches
where we might bog to the ankle,
we learned how to resist that suck and pull
and could stamp in them for fun,
emerging foot-soaked and spattered,
the print of our soles everywhere in the mud,
on the wet doorstep, on the linoleum, on the kitchen floor.

Unapproved Roads

There must have been dozens
cutting through border fields,
of which no one kept track,

or appearing on maps, if at all,
like a fine craquelure
that might have been part of the fabric.

So for miles, there was no border,
just smugglers' routes and stony C roads,
potholed and dangerous.

I imagined a petrol tanker dipping its lights
at the mouth of some nameless turn-off,
and trailers tilting with cigarettes and guns,

and cash changing hands in the country dark beyond
the tarred roads we lived beside, the once-a-day patrols
that kept our lives in order.

Storms

The wind has a million leaves.
Though we have never heard the sea,
in storms the woods are oceanic.

*

Branches crack and one tree has fallen.
If the wind gets loose from the plantation,
the house will capsize.

*

This landscape is all stillness and innocent growth.
It never expected the angry storm-dog
snarling out of the sky.

*

If there are owls in the plantation,
they stay silent and out of sight –
unless their cries are swallowed by the storm.

*

Nature at war. By dawn the casualties
litter the main road, or hang in the trees,
or lie ruined in the fields.

*

The storm is no match for the chestnut tree,
which choreographs every gust as it arrives,
improvises all night.

*

The river in spate, the fields along the river
lakes within hedges. The whole landscape
sodden and out of shape.

*

In less than a minute it is in my eyes,
my hair, my mouth: an apprentice blizzard,
wind-muscled, crazy, packed with the darkness of snow.

Loss of Sound

Thinking of ways he might
express himself,
the Creator turned off
the sound of the snow.
Overnight, the silence of snow
became the silence of the Creator.

The Woodpile

If there were snakes left in Ireland
this is where they would live,
on the sheltered side of the shed,
under an old tarpaulin,
pinned to the ground
by two concrete blocks.
We work our way inwards
all winter
to the centre of the pile,
then outwards again,
the hatchet never done
splitting and trimming,
until at last the woodpile,
down to its first logs, reveals
the spring's pale grasses,
curled and about to uncurl
in even the weakest sunlight,
settling already
into the excitement
of their new skins.

Snowdrop

Somewhere in the snowfield,
the joyous, slow
burial of the snowdrop in the snow.

Landscape with Endangered Species

How were we to know
that the corncrake and the red squirrel
were dying out –
the bush-tailed gymnast shaping his final flourish,
that throat raking the cornfields sick and sore
with the music of last things?

Unfinished Music

Snipe and curlew
fashion on the wing,
unwittingly, in separate languages,
notes towards a definition of place.
They practise, in isolation, the raw sounds
of an appropriate music.
Indifferently, in the long silences, the land
absorbs the echo of
'Dirge for Snipe and Curlew',
which begins again daily and will never be finished.

Towards a Sketch of My Mother

She peers into her brown purse.
I watch her fingers
picking at loose change.

*

I think of her breathing in, a wincing sound.
Smoke whispers from her little sizzling mound
of Potter's Asthma Remedy.

*

A mouth full of clothes pegs, two neat lines
of shirts, jumpers, underwear flapping wetly.
Her thrifty collaboration with the wind.

*

Laid out for burial she embodies,
then disembodies her eighty-three years.
Nothing more to be said of her
that is not in the past tense.
What is said will keep open for a time
the memories through which she will be forgotten.

After a Storm

There is never enough snow.
It falls short always
of the original snow-plain,
the refinement of the last layer,
the soundless, pale settling of the next.

A Zen Dream of Fermanagh

It rained almost daily, almost daily
the rained-on complained. Had we known
about the spirit of Zen we might have gathered
on the Lough shore to welcome the deluge,
chanting refrains to keep, say, intolerance on the move,
if only to the next parish.
I picture whole families practising Zen
in a wet field on the outskirts of Kesh,
or prone by a sacred sheugh
on the road to Belleek.
In my daydream Fermanagh has been named
the first Zen county in Ireland.
We, the denizens, relish the healing cloudburst
and work our watery wiles for the benefit of all.

But to us rainfall was rainfall, bad weather.
The sooner it drained into the earth,
the sooner we were in tune with familiar patterns:
dark clouds, first spittle, the rush for shelter
in a place where it rained almost daily
and almost daily the rained-on complained.

My Father Again

I might have been born to write your elegy.
The moment I lift my pen your soft knock
will be heard at the door. For fifty years or more
you have been my work-in-progress.

I know what brings you here:
the hope that this time
I'll produce a *real* poem –
The Ballad of Paddy Ormsby.
A singer will learn it by heart
and after the to-and-fro
of gruff persuasion and ritual demur,
will hang his cap on his knee, close his eyes,
and sing it to a crowded bar.
It will, you imagine, portray you
as hero of sideline brawls,
the man to have on your side when the fists fly.
Your self-esteem will surely rattle the roof
as the last note of homage fills the room
with whoops and whistles.

But it's my elegy too, half-darkened with loss.
You'll get no ballad this time either.
So again you plunge into the unshaping night.
I slip the latch. Already you are out of sight.

The Farmyard Haiku

1

Tight-arse, waddler,
I astound you
with the perfection of my eggs.

2

Disgruntled in the muck
we will never make music.
Who gives a fuck?

3

I'm Picky, I'm Choosy.
We're the wife's favourites.
She calls us by name.

4

Wattle, glottal, gobble:
we need sub-titles,
even among ourselves.

5

This gander has standards.
You won't catch me
riding my wives in the street.

6

Balls the size of mine
can only be compared
to balls the size of mine.

7

I am the banty rooster. Oversexed?
I'll say! By the way,
you're next.

II

*How one place
can furnish your head and your heart*

The Fisherman

The cowled fisherman
balances up to his waist
at the centre of the Waterworks lake.
How bold was he, how tentative when
he stepped from the shore
and made the world his circle? Now he may cast
extravagantly in every direction.

Taking my retirement for a walk,
I stay to watch him make the first catch.
He raises it to his lips and kisses it,
pout to pout, I imagine, then bends,
custodian of second chances,
to release it, to give it back to itself.

The Black Duckling

Unwittingly, from this angle,
the black duckling sports
a fantail of yellow water lilies.

When she buries her head
and flips her butt in the air
she surrenders the whole ensemble, still unaware.

The Waterworks Park

What do I bring home
from the Waterworks park
where I walk daily?
The same as I leave behind;
voices of waterfowl
with a lot to say,
all of it in the original;
the way water lies always
at the right level;
the heron because of his presence,
the heron because of his absence;
the fishing club camouflaged in their little tents
like a territorial army;
the half-flight of swans, dragging
their feet in the water;
the children pitching crusts
into the dangerous storm of wings;
the undisturbable silence
of the football stadium between matches;
the freewheeling of the Milewater stream
towards its modest whitewater tumble;
the flattest sound in the universe:
the slap of joggers' feet;
the voices of immigrant women
pushing their prams
through a new country;
the water lilies, the bulrushes, the greening sedge;
the thought of how one place
can furnish your head and your heart.
Once more I embark
on the half-hour voyage-in-a-circle,
the inexhaustible mile.

Crows Again

'Too many crows in your poems,
blocking the light.' I can find
only four but, there and then, for her,
I declare a moratorium on crows,
an on-going crow sabbatical,
forbid crows to come within a hundred yards
of any poem by Frank.

An hour later, there are already six
on the rotten fence, not eighty yards away.
The corner-boys of Crow City will slouch
into the nooks of my next poem,
with an air of owning their place.
'You might as well try to exclude death as us.
No poem without crows.'

At the Graveside

We stand in a shy courtesy of loss.
A friend has set out without us, as he must,
on a long journey. No forwarding address.

My Last Words

'It all adds up to whatever it all adds up to.'
Some day, suddenly (if I'm lucky),
I'll simply go out like a light,
without time to say anything,
much less deliver
the spontaneous aphorism
I've already drafted
but has yet to be finalised.

Purgatory

A solemn spirit, neither devil nor angel,
steps forward at the gate and silently hands you
the parcel of your life. It is disappointingly
heavy and tied conclusively
in a way that suggests 'shameful misdemeanours'
or 'the odd mortal sin'. You resist the urge
to administer the drop-kick. A man who died
yesterday should behave with decorum.

Back home, you might leave it in a corner of The Crown
or under the back seat of the Carrs Glen bus,
the number 61 via Cavehill Road. Here it refuses to be set down.
Everyone you encounter has wedged one under an arm,
or tied it to a wrist, or balances it on the head.
Someone has been getting our shit together
all our lives. Now we must carry it indefinitely
like dog-poo, like a ghastly takeaway.

Gunslingers

In Boot Hill Cemetery,
Tombstone, Arizona,
there is a wooden marker:
'Red River Tom,
shot by Ormsby.'

Was the weather to blame,
the pulsing coal of Arizona?
Was it on the crest of a heat wave
that Red River Tom
was shot by Ormsby?

Or was there a woman involved,
a sturdy girl from Tombstone
who drove them both loco?
The upshot: Red River Tom
gets plugged by Ormsby.

Was it a dispute over territory,
Tom baptising himself in the Red River
to stake his claim? His claim lasting
until Ormsby
loaded his rifle.

Whatever the story, it would seem
that Red River Tom
riled one of the ornery
Arizona Ormsbys
and that was the end of him.

For Ciaran Carson

That dapper man in the William Burroughs hat
taking his constitutional in the Waterworks park
could write you a book in six red-hot weeks
when the humour is on him, or tune the tin whistle
to a blackbird theme, or descant on the art of translation.
For two decades the Eglantine Inn
was our spiritual, or for you, Ciaran, spirituous home,
poetry one of the fervours of our lives,
our mad desire to capture nothing less
than the perfect lyric.
On smoky nights dense with acerbic judgements,
you wagged your nicotined finger in our faces
and stammered what was fantastic,
what was mad dog's shite, our soundtrack,
the air conditioning, beginning to roar
like the engines of the Liverpool Ferry.
Maps and Mallarmé, hurling, traditional song,
Belfast as a waterbed city born in the sea.
If this were a film, I'd have you appear and
disappear among the entries of the old city,
or take on yourself the street identities:
the man who balanced the cardboard box
on his head along Royal Avenue,
or Buck Alec walking his lion, or a small angry man –
no shortage of those – talking to himself or cursing his dog.
And, Deirdre, if the man you know as husband
produces a gun and offers to shoot an apple
off your head, it's time to run, Deirdre, run.

Lunch in The Crown with Michael Longley

Autumnal light kindles the goddess Fortuna
on a stained glass window. First snug on the right.
Bangers and mash and an exchange of new poems.
Our thirty-year friendship
enjoys, at last, a post-war ripening –
though we are, perhaps, too quick to award ourselves
the Medal of Perseverance because we stayed
through decades of others' bloodshed and plied our trade
in offices and classrooms.
We've kept the poems coming, for what they are worth,
add small stones to the cairns of love and sorrow, rejoice
in whatever has not been blown to pieces.
Have we any choice but to go on greeting
the birth of grandchildren with a poetry of prayers and wishes,
or sit down in peacetime, under Fortuna, to eat and talk.
So it's bangers and mash again, with sweet gravy –
elemental pig-and-potato stuff
that keeps us grounded. Next the ritual exchange
of poems, mine a ten-liner about boyhood
in which my father dies for the fifteenth time,
yours, a three-line epic on a Mayo otter
crossing the *duach*, words that have kept
you sleepless half the night.

An Evening in The John Hewitt with Conor Macauley

Mad for a pint of Hoegaarden, I ring my friend.
A bus ride later, the two of us converge
on The John Hewitt. We settle. We extend
four decades, rich, we believe, in talk and alcohol
and a charged silence peculiarly our own.
The bar-room light changes hour by hour,
like the genial rasp of a hundred opinions.
Far be it from us to scorn that blatherdom
of things trying to get said, then said again.
A cruise ship has docked in Belfast for the day
and the last ashore are rubber-necking past,
their cameras crammed with shots of the miracle city
getting up from its ruins. How we have come to care,
not for the Belfast tucked in *Titanic* dreams,
but the wounded city healing after a war!
Now, as the lights dim, we gather images,
for the home journey:
logs settling in their ash, a bar clock's chime,
among old photographs, a bar tender calling time.

Visiting the Grave

We visit your grave on weekdays, you who dressed
the ordinary weekday in its Sunday best
and the weekday heart of Sunday taking its rest.

Grandfather's Week

'I never want to read another poem by an Irish poet, in
which his grandfather enters or emerges from a shed.'

On Monday Grandfather visits his shed
at least twice. He carries what looks like
blackout curtains, a sizeable chandelier
and a case of Bud Lite.

On Tuesday he is a one-man stream of traffic.
Into the shed go maps of all the oceans,
a telescope, numerous buckets of black earth
and a crate of Guinness.

On Wednesday he tips ten wheelbarrows
of cut grass in a corner of the shed,
fits in a small apple tree with fruit on the branches
and six bottles of fruity Australian red.

Surely no room for more. But on Thursday
the shed roof creaks open like a convertible's
to make room for huge replicas of Sun and Moon
and an array of cocktails with parasols.

Imagine the chaos on Friday when he coaxes
a garden full of wild beasts and creeping things
into a shed that seems to expand invisibly
when he clicks his fingers. So much dark rum,

so much cider to pack on Saturday,
he fetches a man and woman to complete the task
and take up residence in the shed.
Their work finished, on Sunday they drink all day.

Small World (3)

Synchronised lift-off. Two white swans
happy-slapping
the Waterworks lake.

*

Always invisible
the precise second
when the first flake takes hold.

*

Ten thousand leaves have gone
to ground in the garden.
Beloved autumn!

*

Under the dripping stone
a bulbous frog
straight from the Tang Dynasty.

*

The meadow grass after a March shower –
let's call it
Irish Spring Green.

The Snail

What were you thinking?
You are halfway up our door,
with your little mosque on your back
and still going strong.
Has the moon's glint on the letterbox
gone to your head?
Where will you turn
at the top of the white mountain?

The Soul

I thought of it as a neat parcel, somehow alive,
in a soul-cupboard in my chest, or a stylish drawer-for-the-soul.
If alive, did it sleep at night? Or was it condemned
to lug our sins behind it like ponderous chains?

Older, I understood, or thought I did,
the soul's dilemmas – an immortal trapped
among the imperfect,
suffering too the melancholy of exile,
and stuck with us as its best shot at Heaven.

Now, when I think of my soul, it registers first
as 'soul' in the abstract. Then at the corner of my eye,
the shifting shape of a gigantic amoeba surfaces
in what looks like its personal ocean. Or a huge sea-blossom
that is also a fish, blooms with a flourish, briefly.
My soul, whatever it is, is too good for me
and full of surprises. Clean as on the day I was born,
it seems to exude a dense, genial shimmer.
But whether it is scattering eggs, just now, or seeds,
or dancing to sweet soul-music, damned if I know.

The Cult

Midnight on the appointed day
and the world has not ended.

In the field where they have gathered
dawn survives its customary pallor.

The prophet's book lies open at the page
where the calculations of a life-time

have produced the wrong answer. Now the believers need
someone to joke that it's not the end of the world,

to say their children will live after all and that they
have tasted reprieve – however hard to imagine

the shabby, continuing days, the long let-down
of a planet that failed to explode.

Meanwhile, they face the entrance to the field
as though that were the likeliest spot

for conclusive omens. The Leader will storm through
with his leadership voice, his magnetic leadership eyes –

unless the rumours are true that he has absconded
with his PA and the No Tomorrow Fund.

Noon and the earth keeps going, cattle at the fence
gawping and swishing their tails.

The followers with no one to follow, feeling the cold
and with no plans for the evening, set out

in search of stew and sandwiches. They begin to conceive
of doubt as a condition. They no longer know what to believe.

Outside The Walls

Those poor little bastards
in their shoe-box coffins,
in their unmarked graves.

After Edward Hopper: *Sun in an Empty Room*

Bare as it is, this room has history.
The last tenants went
and took their shadows with them,
the next are due to bring their own
small shadows, such as are cast by lamps,
and vases and clocks and framed photographs and chairs.

Something about the shapes and colours
makes me think of empty suitcases,
the ancient brown ones lined
with newspaper. Someone faceless
is speeding across a bridge towards
the tatters of a new beginning, someone glad
of shadows and angled windows and sunlight, however cold.

No Telling

No telling what has arrived here
in the night: red dust from the Sahara,
volcanic ash from the heart of Iceland,
salting and peppering the topsoil
on both sides of the Lough.

A passenger ship from Europe docks in the dark
over a hundred years ago, Jewish families gripping the rails
and lugging as much of the old life as might be pressed
into a few cases, say, and travelling bags.

The mist behind is a curtain
closing on the past, the mist ahead
a damp drapery that begins to unfold
the new life, the fresh start, the clean freedoms –
if they can ever again
be at home in one place.

Elsewhere, a flake of meteorite
detached from the night sky,
silts into the dark bed
of a country lake.
The ripples settle quickly.
It will never be found.

Belfast Needs Fountains

Belfast needs fountains, bubblers and gushers,
sprinklers and white water torrents and frothy monsoons,
joyous fountainy stallions leaping in air
and falling back dramatically and swallowing themselves;
and watercress fountains and stylish fountains
quiffed like a Hokusai wave,
and deodorant fountains in a fragrant fog,
dancing fountains, harmless-mad-bastard fountains
waiting to wet you through and rain-forest fountains
drenching and dowsing and deluging and brimming over.
And big incontinent fountains, orifices awash from dawn to dusk.

So the whole city would be symphonic with water,
baptised and eroticised and water-empowered,
its scores of fountains filling with wet coins
and charged with the granting of wishes.
Trips to the City Centre would open the soul
to the sound of water, our best selves picking light
off freshwater streams from the hills, our best dreams
becoming a cleansing inland tide in a city of fountains.

III

TWENTY-SIX IRISH PAINTINGS

Let them have rooms with big windows.
Make them restless for the world but not unhappy.

1 Aloysius O'Kelly: *The Christening Party*

Family and friends have gathered in the pub
to wet the baby's head. Judging by their demeanour
they have been here for some time. The sound level
in the painting is as close as silence comes
to shattering the barrier of the inaudible.
The plump woman with her back to us is pacing herself,
glass, three-quarters full, propped on her knee
under the table, within sipping distance.
Her companion has flung his arms wide
to embrace the company. They are all of one mind.
The child's mother is wording the toast
and the glasses are raised in the right direction.
Soon Aunt Francoise will be as full as a tick.
Uncle Louis' glass is empty, as are his eyes.
He accepts a stiff refill from a man
with a hand on his shoulder that might be brotherly,
or a controlling weight, or death by alcohol.
As for the baby, she may remember all this
as the Night of the Crazies in their crazy hats,
and the clinking of glasses and the incomprehensible din
and the little barred window and her vantage point
in the crook of her mother's arm.
I wish I knew what they are drinking and what
name the child was given that day in 1908
and how she fared in the next decade of a bloody century,
much of the blood local. Set hindsight aside,
accept that the moment shows her loved and protected.
The chance to flourish may be the luck of her dear life,
whatever we might imagine, whatever fear.

2 John Lavery: *Under the Cherry Tree*

1

Father, if that is indeed Father, is pencil slim
and nattily dressed and he punts with a certain panache.
Whether he has just landed or is preparing to go,
he stands in the boat, perfectly balanced,
like a gondolier on holiday. You expect him
to raise his straw boater and take a bow.
When he kisses his wife and daughter, his lips taste
of afternoon drinks with the artists.

2

If he is showing off, Mother is posing
thoughtfully against a dodgy fence by the water.
She is queen of the wheelbarrow and the watering can.
Her breasts are a bold statement and her strong arms.
She is about to stretch like a cat and will then revert
to being a gardener. Somehow she takes possession
of this part of the river, just by looking at it.
She owns Father too, more subtly than he knows.

3

The girl is young and has her back to us
and is, it would seem, an only child.
She is the future, which is why her gaze
is fixed on Mother. Mother is what she will be.
We imagine for her the kind of prettiness
that goes with bonnets and plain dresses and plaited hair.
'We'd be mad to leave this place,' she is thinking.
She sits cross-legged on the barrow, secure as you please.

4

There is work for the barrow and the watering-can
among ugly, misshapen growths, in the parched earth
that burnishes the foreground.
They promise hours of sweat and broken nails.
The wheelbarrow with the big wheel
and the gigantic watering-can
seem scaled to reclaim the river-bank
for grass and cherry trees and the bourgeoisie.

5

There is nothing grievous here, except the knowledge
such beauty cannot last. On a day like this
the thought would break your heart. That sad sense
of endless summers ending. The harm will be done
in the course of a day's rough showers,
the river swollen after heavy rain and hungry for petals,
the wind plucking exquisite blossoms and blowing them away,
their short lives, lost in the currents, bobbing to a close.

3 Walter Osborne: *Apple Gathering, Quimperlé*

Weep for the green orchards of northern France
before the two world wars, their apple-rich largesse
bound ripely to the sap and to the sun
in fertile villages. At Quimperlé,
two girls are harvesting a tree bent sideways
by the weight of apples, one wielding a long stick
to bring them to earth, the other in her wake,
bending to gather. Just now their backs are turned
to the blockish bell-tower on the hill.
They seem composed in their rough working clothes,
and are aiming to fill that barrow with a fresh
cargo of apples. The promise of baking and brewing
is a scent in the air, and the prospect of rest,
after, say, one more tree, is partly what keeps them going.
Each of them will wipe an apple on her dress
and close her eyes and eat it slowly
until the ringing of the angelus bell
sets them moving to the next tree. Now their work has a taste,
now they can taste the work of the orchard
and will soon, for all we know, begin to sing
as their arms resume stretching.
Weep for the green orchards of northern France
before the two world wars...

4 Stanley Royle: *The Goose Girl*

Admit it, my posture and the posture of my geese
impresses you, not to mention the accessories –
bag, bonnet, stick, the short-sleeved,
ground-length orange dress I know
will turn heads. Everything about me
and my charges is alert and purposeful.
They know where we are going and stretch ahead,
I am straight-backed as the trees that sunbathe
in their lakes of bluebells. The cut flowers
I carry in my bag will grace a small flower-pot
at my mother's door.

Whatever is meant, exactly, by a sense of place, here
includes her slender presence. This neck of the woods
may be said to be hers in a way it is not mine.
It begins to be mine as I watch her glide through,
all the more lovely for the homage of the cut flowers,
beauty acknowledging beauty, and the stately geese
and the bluebells at her feet and the sunshine
coming towards her through the trees.

5 Norman Garstin: *Among the Pots*

You can always find uses for a decent pot.
What pot-orientated lives we seem to lead,
to judge by the display and the expected demand
in the village market. It's wall to wall
earthenware in reds and maroons on a cobbled street
in Brittany. One woman, seated, completes the paperwork,
or dreams up a slogan or a Special Offer.
Another bends to finish a display. From here,
they don't have the look of a dynamic sales force,
but give them a chance to talk you through their wares
and your pot-holdings may increase by a container for apples,
a pot for Madonna lilies, a cask for home brew,
a tasteful pot-shaped funeral urn to be kept in an outhouse.
The background fills with potential customers,
the awnings are down, the pots catching the sunlight.
Pot sales in Brittany are about to go through the roof.

6 Norman Garstin: *Madonna Lilies*

Madonna lilies, nuns among flowers,
nuns of the middle air,
a stand of them in blossom
enough to prompt the sign of the Cross,
enough to set poems ringing.
Attracted, infatuated, I stop just short
of naming you 'religio-erotic'.
But religio-erotic you are,
temptresses every one,
yet filling me with the idea
of purity.
Girls of the middle air,
you have set me babbling,
lovely girls, mistresses every one.
Sensuous blooms
of the religio–erotic
madonna lilies.

7 Joseph Malachy Kavanagh: *Pursuing His Gentle Calling*

Homesick for Brittany, I don my Breton beret
and pick my spot in a snowy Dublin street.
Five minutes, no more, to balance the easel,
open the case of paints and squat on my portable seat.
Ah, the restless joys of pursuing my gentle calling!
No sooner have I lit my pipe and set my brush to work
than here he comes again, the Breton peasant
who limps through my etching 'On the Ramparts: Mont St Michel'
and 'The Old Convent Gate, Dinand'. That was four years ago.
Once more he has his back to me and is walking away.
I recognise the stick, the hat, the bag crossways
on his breast. This time I will cross it to the right.
He is there in the way your dead father might surface
and oblige you to lose and bury him over and over.
Again I have left it late, not painting him first
but catching the buildings ahead. If I'm not quick about it,
he'll be round the corner and something unfinished
will continue, for better or worse, to skirt completion.
As it will anyway. Next time I'll spread the snows of Dublin,
the snows of Brittany around his feet.
I will cure his limp and fill a pipe for him.
He will turn his back on me. He will walk away.

How objects, even when ordered, can clutter a room,
command the illusion there is nothing we cannot have,
that, in fact, what we own already defines success.
Feel free to envy the display of plates, pans,
pottery, empty vases, cutlery, fabrics,
the wicker clothes-basket, the exotic tablecloth,
the sumptuous green arras. No wonder the sisters
are taking time out with the few tattered pages
that affirm there are lives elsewhere.
The little sister's arm around
her big sister's shoulder revises delicately
the room's hierarchy of values,
as does their serious heads-together perusal
of the small print, in which the intricacies
of the room are, at least for the present, forgotten.

What will the sisters do next? Cut out dress patterns,
or travel news, or a paragraph from the society pages
about someone they know?
Let them find a clutter-free corner for their clippings –
that bare patch of wall, for example, under the shelf
is a display board in the making.
Let them have rooms with big windows.
Make them restless for the world but not unhappy.

9 Walter Osborne: *Breton Girl by a River*

She prefers to pose in an orchard, as she did
in 'Apple Gathering, Quimperlé'. An orchard's the place
to be if you're hungry and bored. Still, her new patch
by the river is not without interest. It has the look
of a ramshackle shrine, with steps as to an altar,
and is roofed with uneven boards, as though the painter
had dragged from the river a flotsam-and-jetsam
backdrop for his study of the Breton girl.
She carries a bowl. He has set a jug at her feet
so that she is not passive, has brought offerings
as the river brings itself to the base of the wall
and the foliage descends to green-hat the loose boards
roofing that redbrick folly. The sun is shining here.
The girl is in no danger. She is the French model
from the 1880s that we do not get to know:
the patient Breton, the washerwoman, the apple-gatherer,
the Normandy wife. What does she make of the artists
who lodge all summer in the villages along the river?
What does she make of that hunger to catch her world
on canvas, the luminosity that is not just light,
but light and water, light and foliage, light and sky,
light falling on faces? No reason this girl should think
of her own face looking out freshly after a hundred and forty years,
and ours looking in, as though we might,
in other circumstances, break into speech,
manage, in broken English, in broken French,
a sentence or two worth saying.

10 Roderic O'Conor: *Portrait of a Young Woman Smiling*

'I'm over here,' the artist must have said.
'Look at me and smile.' Instantly that smile
broke on her face, a most tremendous gift,
and the artist painted a portrait of the smile
and the young woman held it as only a natural
smile can hold. The lifetime of a smile
informs its newest blossoming.
A face full of happiness comes with happiness lived.
Nothing dulled or oppressed or flirtatious
about this smile. The artist must be smiling too.

11 May Guinness: *Pump at Pont-l'Abbé*

The round table with the pointed roof
at the centre of the village square
has me dizzy with local history.
Which, in these parts, is the world history
of two wars and the long conflicts of Europe.
A closer look would show the stonework chipped
by gunfire where the local freedom fighters
took cover, or the village collaborators
fell, blindfolded, at the base. Some of the lovers
who went public can still shadow-
write their initials in the crumbling plaster.
The pump attached to the wall is inexhaustible,
a cold, deep gushing that has never failed
villager or traveller or militia man
or the horses on market day. Think of processions
that have circled it at Christmas and Easter,
or the chasing games of children,
or the dancing rites of adolescents,
and round them, at a distance,
the pagan circlings of whatever stood there
before the tower. If I were in Pont-l'Abbé
I would join the queue for water, cup
in my hands that cold source
for as long as it let me and think
of the last mouthful as spirit of Brittany,
essence of Pont-l'Abbé.

I was out, as is my wont, at Barbizon,
feeding the pigeons, most of them little fatties
chasing for bread and smugly content to be grounded.
When all of a sudden a pair I had not seen
appeared in the air above me. Setting their whiteness
against the background of a dark thicket,
they offered a circling routine of loops and floatings
and playful preambles. God forgive
my sudden flash of the Angel Gabriel
bringing his news... 'Oh, don't be ridiculous,'
I told myself and went to turn away
and fling the last crusts to my flabbies.
When all of a sudden I thought of *him*, the one
I miss, but to whom I have never spoken, who keeps me awake
and haunts my waking hours. And I looked again
at the two pigeons, hoping they would land
to eat my bread and feed my fantasy,
but they were not our omen – unless perhaps they were.
Meanwhile, a squabble had broken out
between Fat Head and Friar Tuck and I shooed them off.
By then the two pigeons had flown away
and I hadn't the heart to sweep up the leavings.
'Oh, don't be ridiculous,' I told myself
when all of a sudden...

13 Stanhope Forbes: *Miss Ormsby, later Mrs Homan*

I met Miss Ormsby on her way to the studio
to sit for Stanhope Forbes. She stopped to talk –
the kind of talk that goes with an open face,
intelligent eyes and – I flatter myself – a trust in the listener.
She had toured the galleries, studying the portraits of women.
'Dulled and unsmiling' was the phrase she used,
whether society wives, or working girls, or Breton peasants,
or dancers, or mothers with their children.
They hardly ever looked directly at the painter.
Were they really so passive? And were these matters
she might broach with Mr Forbes? She is to marry
young Homan and joked about losing her name.
I agreed that Ormsby was a melodious name,
a mellifluous name, a name you could set to music,
but assured her that Homan was solid and promised much:
the weight of the dependable, for example,
and a domesticated husband. Warmed and stimulated
by this agreeable nonsense, we said our farewells.
Months later, when I saw the portrait, she was not smiling
but a smile was in the offing. She was direct
and lively in her way and lovely. Something ascetic there also.
The painter, lifted by his subject, had missed nothing –
the hair, the eyebrows, the white, three-flowered brooch,
worn as though she might be a member
of a confident new order. Young Mr Homan
will have his work cut out. Lucky, lucky Mr Homan.

The woman burning leaves may dream tonight
of herself feeding the flames, half-cradling in her lap
what she has gathered for the burning.
Her eyes are on the fire but her face is closed
around the moment pensiveness gives way
to small miseries. She is tidying up
the landscape of her life.
You can tell she has secrets that, despite her care,
will show in her face among the low houses.
Those roofs and gables at her back are well grounded
in all the seasons, so too the russet fence
at the bottom of what must be her back garden.
But even these blur to reflections
in the village pond. The bonfire smokes leaf-brown,
highlights the cold sky travelling this way,
full of night and winter.

15 William John Leech: *Convent Garden, Brittany*

She walks with God all right, the white-clad nun
in Leech's picture, who breezes past everyone
and everything in the convent garden.
She moves, eyes blindly open, towards an elsewhere
that only she, afloat on her holiness, can discern.
Around her the flowers are turning gorgeous
in a different rapture, her sisters absorbed
in hanging their washing out while the sun shines.
Only Sister Olympia, it seems, has a rendezvous.
She is hurrying out of the picture and we,
caught in her vision and hustled into choice,
are tempted to hurry after.

Why the long face, the lugubrious mien?
That's the latest trend, that's how the painters
and public want their clowns. I paint my smile
daily with a downward droop, so it stops
being a smile and seems to mourn all through
my act. The world is an absurd place,
I grant you that. People are absurd.
I'm expected to confirm this, reflect it
in comic turns that skirt unhappiness.
I am not, in any case, a happy fellow.
I squat in the well of my trousers
and play the buffoon and half look forward
to my clown therapy with a scented candle
and the sympathetic eyes of the painter.
My palms rise to my cheeks
as though to direct the candle's heat
into a caress. I look older without the cosmetics
but am more myself and may yet
have a laugh when the painter least expects it.
I tell her that my best friend is grey to the soul,
five tons of ennui with an angst so deep
you can see it in his feet. No, not the ringmaster,
I mean the elephant. Beside him,
I'm a barrel of laughs. If there isn't a word
for loneliness in crowds, there ought to be.
And a word for the silence so full
it might be despair or communion.
I am in and out of the shadow where I sit
with my hands raised and my elbows on the table.
Does the set of my mouth remember its last smile
and fashion the next? Is there a place
beyond sympathy where I take the prize
for the painter's most depressing subject ever?
Self-pity, if you will, but I can't help reflecting
that in this country they light candles for the dead.

17 Frank O'Meara: *On the Quays, Étaples*

What wintry impulse, what bleak patch in her soul
brings Grandmother to the quays? Only a storm
would rule out her favourite mile of land edge
and shifting, unreadable sky. Into the mist,
out of the mist, the boatmen ferry
the day's travellers. Her granddaughter hangs
on her arm, full of questions and chat,
so that grey is less dense than it was,
and, in the harbour, outlines shape up and horizon
is more than a rumour. Then Grandmother prevails,
her daily walk a serious rehearsal.
Cheerful is not appropriate.
The policy here is heads down in dim sea-light.
Into the mist, out of the mist, the boatmen
help passengers aboard, commit in silence
to whatever they are about
on this wintry coast, in their semi-visible world.

18 Henry Jones Thaddeus: *The Wounded Poacher*

It is as though Christ at the foot of the Cross
is still alive and instinctively makes for home,
blood dripping from the wound in his shoulder,
pain re-drawing the lineaments of his face,
until he collapses into the sturdy chair
in front of the fire and passes out.
He drops his head back into his wife's tenderness,
mouth open unconsciously as though to kiss.
Already she has stripped him to the waist.
He is twice caressed, her hand on his shoulder,
the sponge soothing and cleaning the shoulder-wound.
Forgotten just now the violence of the night,
though it fills the room – the gun dropped at his feet,
the tumbled chair, the scatter of garments,
the dead creatures shrivelling on the floor.
She will take his boots off, hoping he'll set aside
the dangerous life at last, or at least stay the night,
though she knows she will wake in the small hours to find
the bed half-empty, to imagine the ticking woods
and the call of his fugitive night-work
beyond pain or comfort. She will think of him up with the lark,
bandaged, impenitent, still shading into the dark.

19 Frank O'Meara: *The Widow*

The widow walks by the river, in black and alone,
the wind undoing her veil. She is hanging
on nobody's arm, seems to stand free
of family and friends. Now she is here,
will she test herself against the first loneliness?
Or adjust to the bereavement space
in which she is the chief mourner?
Intense memory has closed her eyes.
She wants a river in her grief and bare trees
and little low islands, a geography of loss, a local scene
where distances conflict and horizons give back nothing.
She is marked, if she allows it, a widow for life.
Monsieur O'Meara, a painter with a taste
for the *lacrimae rerum*, an aficionado of Autumn and Winter,
has asked her to pose. He has taken her arm
courteously and complicated her sadness.
He will complicate it again with the finished portrait.

Taking a rest from people and finding the yard
favoured by sunlight, the artist falls in love,
not for the first time, with the outhouse clutter
of brick and wood. Suddenly it seems important
to record those two doors into the dark,
the rough ladder propped against the wall,
hens scrounging in that irritating way
that invites you to trip over them.
The greenery climbing the wall is in need of a trim.
Allowed to flourish, then spreading out of control,
it threatens the ladder. The workers may be having a nap,
or sitting to eat somewhere behind the artist.
I imagine him chewing bread, a doorstop wedge
that leaves seeds between his teeth and make conversation
almost impossible. I imagine him drinking wine
when he stops to think, and how he will attend
to light and shadow, and the difference
one brushstroke will make.

21 William John Leech: *Interior of a Barber's Shop*

The universe is male and requires a hair-cut
once a month. When the universe is silent,
it is amassing its next utterance,
which will be beyond argument.
When the universe speaks, the universe has spoken.
Somewhere there is a bag of clippings, mostly grey,
to be consigned to the fire. Soon it will contain
the thinnings from the present customer,
the barber's sheet wrapping him like a shroud.
His hair will have started growing again before
the last strands settle on the floor.
His hair will go on growing after his death.

My surly delinquent, the boldest of the bold!
She worked where I lodge
at the Hôtel de l'Europe, in the village of Concale.
That's how she came to lean against a wall
in the foreground of my *Street in Brittany*.
There are eight other women in the street,
but I have eyes only for her moody sleepwalker's face,
her faintly desperate grip
on the stuffed animal for which she seems too old.
Last week she lost her employment at the hotel,
dismissed for stealing I don't know what, a few coins.
All out of character, or so it seemed,
until this week, when she demanded payment
from me – and the painting barely begun. She knew
I needed her to bring that street alive.
So we quarrelled to an agreement and she withdrew
into herself, looking at no one as no one
looked at her, pondering perhaps the follies
of her life in one short week. Just now she is tense and subdued,
her clogs at attention, stiff as army boots,
though when I say so there is no answering smile.
Has her spirit taken a knock? I cannot tell.
She will sit for me again, for few can bring
such natural feeling, such challenge to the bare canvas.
In the autumn, my imp, my urchin, our paths divide.
What will become of you? A fisherman's wife?
The scourge of the French coast? I want to count the ways
your life might flourish, though troubles haunt your door.
In the meantime, scowl if you will,
the sunlight in this painting will be all yours.

She is a worrier. You can tell by the way she leans
forward in her chair and aims her stare
across the table, directly into his face.
She wills him to close his newspaper,
take off his boater and hear what she has to say.
He continues turning the pages. Such pointed indifference
presages rows and storms and bursts of tears
that will carry into the street. Their small unhappiness,
if unhappiness is ever small, flares
daily between them. She will sit here as long as she must,
he will make a show of failing to notice.
Like figures who have slipped
from the centre of a portrait,
they languish in a corner. Soon, as is their wont,
they will merge again into the quarrel of their lives,
which is nobody's business but theirs.
When he finishes the sports pages, she will be at hand
to follow him out. His pace, though not at first,
will adjust to hers. If not passion, tolerance.
If not love itself, the heat like a buried coal
that has somehow not burnt out.
They will commit, for now, to a misery they understand.

24 Richard Thomas Moynan: *The Laundress*

I

The laundress is young, and active and all attention
to cuffs and collars and the white sleeve that falls
over the edge of the table. She is half-sanctified
by the way her head seems printed on the white pillow-case,
then humanised by the neat bun of her hair.
We cannot avoid the eyes of her pale companion,
the fair-haired girl with face propped in hand
and elbow on the table- ennui itself, so close
to the iron she is almost in the way.
The eyes look out of the picture with a kind of wisdom.
Is it that she cannot bear to age into the life
prefigured in this basement room? Is her dream to escape
the basket of dirty linen, the two brass pitchers,
the clothes-line, the pendulum on the wall?
Or is she impatient to be herself
the queen laundress, the one in charge?

II

Meanwhile, the shirt hanging upside down on the line
might be playing the spirit of the wash
while the humanoids are not looking.
The Master has worn him out. 'Not you again,'
the laundresses groan, caressing his wrinkled skin.
He favours outdoor drying in a flirtatious breeze
over this indoor rigor mortis, especially when the audience includes
four black socks and what looks like an exotic
tablecloth he has not seen before.

25 Nathaniel Hone: *Old Woman Gathering Sticks*

No one to help this morning. The thin trees stand round
like a gathering of brittle bones. Their arms suggest
a series of exercises that will keep her warm.
But the old woman is shaking last night's snow
off fallen branches, the faggots on her back
in part the debris of last year's storms. We trust her cottage
is not far off and that the shining band of sky
on the horizon is arriving, not departing.
To look for and glimpse later the smoke from her chimney
would be a winter gift. Just now, her survival skills
are at work on a handful of kindling
and she is looking up, her head wrapped
in what might be a bandage or a stylish new turban,
bought with the thaw in mind and the onset of spring.

A peasant girl comes smiling out of the woods,
bringing the whole spring with her and finding
the whole spring waiting in the artist's welcome.
They manage the illusion of a surprise meeting.
while, above, the sky opens
a surprising umbrella of light.
She stands as in a doorway, so that, through her,
the natural world becomes accessible
in more than externals. For as long
as she stands there, the spring intensifies
in one place. If she poses much longer the trees
will bend an arch of homage and protection
over her head. We, too, are reduced to saplings,
in love again with quotidian pleasures,
the modest stuff of beauty and abundance.

IV

THE PARKINSON'S POEMS

The false distances
between us and all harm.

Agitans

My left arm is jealous of my right,
the one without a tremor. When Right
pours a glass of wine or throws a ball,
Left stifles a mild shiver of reproach.
I call him Agitans and let him take charge
of the big jug of water, so that the ice
tumbles into the glasses like a subsiding cliff.
He peaks in the football season when Arsenal play.
If they get any better, I'll have to snuggle him
tightly to my chest, strait-jacket style.
Meanwhile, his brother Right is undeterred
by his burgeoning duties. And once, once only,
has released his own answering tremor.

Tremors

Not the tremors themselves
but what the tremors portend:
craters swallowing the city,
the mine collapsing,
the cliff-face toppling into the sea.

Also some fault in the self
that will go on opening
for as long as we live
and cannot be repaired.

Side Effects (1)

> Hallucinations may be among the side effects
> of some medications...

Wherever I sit, at the corner of my eye,
they fade-in-fade-out, melt into elsewhere
before I can see faces. Who is that girl
I sense at my shoulder? Who is that dancing lazily
on my table until I look up?
Are they playing a game? Do they mean me any harm?

Not one has appeared twice or uttered a sound.
Remote, indifferent, they will never amount
to a family or a circle of friends.

Meanwhile, a black spider with his heart in his mouth
is legging it across the floor-tiles towards the nearest shade.
He is strangely human and visible all the way.

Notes in Small Handwriting

Thank you for the list of symptoms.
I have them all.
Also for the postcard photo
of spring leaves dripping
at the end of a bough.
That too I recognise.

*

A tremor centuries old
'paralysis agitans'
'the Shaking Palsy'
'Parkinson's Disease'.
Poignant as any poppy
its emblematic flower:
the red tulip.

*

My brother and I at a wedding:
enough tremors between us
to rival the air-conditioning.

*

Early stages:
the decorous blur of the plural,
the false distances
between us and all harm.

The Insulin Pen

Star-struck by Parkinson's, its visible shake
and public profile, ludicrously in thrall
to the cheap glamour of hallucinations,
have you forgotten me, your not-so-old,
Novomix 30 pen? Once you thought me
'more precious than a hip-flask',
lighter than loose change, a true blood-brother.
You declared me at international airports
and stored me in cool places, carried me, God knows why,
on hunger-trips to that strip of Cavehill Road
with the off-licence and six takeaways –
you called it 'Death Row'.
And what of our dash to hospital, the Coke binges,
the mad, unslakable thirst?

I claim you for diabetes. We got you first.

Hallucinations (1)

Why are they not more brash, more lively,
these creatures who live in my head –
a troop of Ariels, say, or some nifty *cirque du soleil*
acrobats and clowns? Instead,
they pass in a blur, trying to be seen
trying not to be seen.
I may never be rid of them, though
leavetaking seems their speciality. They zip away
out of lamps, statues, vases, cushions, chairs,
but without the words or gestures.
I want them to slow down once in a while,
unsmiling if they will, but they are too busy time-flying.
Rashness or liveliness are not, I guess, their style.

Even as I write, discreetly, deliberately,
something hustles out of sight at the gable's edge.
That its very presence may be bad news
bounces me to my feet. I stride in the garden,
then work on an image of lights malfunctioning
and light-doctors on overtime
hurrying to make repairs.

Hallucinations (2)

So used to them have I become,
so aware without thinking
of their nameless presence
and their ways of peopling a room,
I spoke absently to the one lurking
in my mother-in-law's chair
and called it Jean and asked
about holiday plans.
When I looked in its direction it disappeared.
Not much conversation to be shared
with a neurological disturbance.
Everyone else in the room, if indeed anybody
else was there, remained invisible.
And a loneliness beyond reason began to take hold.
And things impossible lost themselves again
in a round of regrets.
There was no breakthrough, there was no
crossing of lines.

Hallucinations (3)

My silent visitors
wouldn't startle a mouse,
so still they sit, sometimes,
on every chair in the conservatory.
They might be teachers or civil servants
with a taste for line-dancing
and Country music.
At times they exude
a kind of homelessness,
displaced beings
crashing at my pad.
They have the fearsome
patience of invalids.
Whatever it is they are waiting for,
they will wait forever.

Friends

Which would you rather have,
Parkinson's or Alzheimer's?
Parkinson's. I'd rather spill half my pint
than forget where the hell I put it down.

When I am disposed
to make room for a mild depression
or cite the medical history
of the tremor in my left arm,
they shout me down
with 'shaker' jokes and quotations.
I call them heartless bastards
but begin to accept requests.
My party piece is called;
'The Plane in the Storm'.
Then I'm allowed
the last quotation –
from Yeats's poem
in praise of his friends
and charged with lump-in-the-throat
desire for the woman he loves.
He describes how sweetness
wells from his heart's root.
'I shake,' Yeats tells us,
'I shake from head to foot.'

Side Effects (2)

Gone my teacherly gulder. All you allow
on the worst days is an adolescent scrake.
The voice that broke at thirteen has again
broken. Mad Sweeney in the trees
might have sounded like this.

Farewell to the dulcet and the mellifluous,
though, in truth, they were never my style.
Now, reading aloud, I clear my throat between poems
that words may have right of way,
or return patiently to where the sound was scrambled,
each lost syllable recovered, given its say.

Side Effects (3)

Alone in the house, I fart to the slow movement
from Rimsky-Korsakov's *Capriccio Espagnol*,
the dazzling 'Morning Dance'.

I set aside Vivaldi's *Concerto for Two Trumpets
in C major*, bought at the Oxfam sale.
Tomorrow shines. Who knows what heights I may scale?

Once a Day

I take my hallucinations for a walk
once a day at the Waterworks, that is to say
I assume they accompany me.
Acres of fresh air, some trees, a lake –
plenty of space to practise disappearing.
Would the dogs detect an aura or take a snarl
at the invisible? I expected not.

I expected right. Park life has its own concerns.
The heron gathers North around him
like a monk's habit and appears to sleep.
The 'Joggers Against Oblivion' are already
on a gasping break. Only the terrier,
Stupid Fucker, draws near and growls, then
turns to the more urgent business of his life,
chasing a ball for the angriest man in Ireland.

The Later Stages (1)

That lively man
in the wheelchair
could be me,
ten years from now,
abroad in the Waterworks park,
a tremor in both arms,
and giving the nod
to trees, lake, dog-walkers and waterfowl.
I will praise the people I love
who still love me. I will celebrate
the waterbirds' barbaric music.
My visionary companions
will still be around. Lurking
indoors and out, not once
will they have broken cover long enough
for a face to take shape.
When you ask how I'm doing,
I'll tell you the one
about 'parking zones disease'.
I'll assure you that the pills seem to be working.

The Later Stages (2)

You may leave me that
I cannot lace a shoe,
or button a shirt,
or handle a knife and fork,
or plant snowdrops,
or trim a garden hedge,
or climb a ladder,
or drive my wife to work.

I may learn patience,
but reserve the right
to rail against you.
Assuming I'm alive,
expect an outburst
once a year at least,
a tantrum at seventy,
a rant at seventy-five.

V

THE WILLOW FOREST

I think of the places where the truth was lost.

The Accused (1)

At the War Tribunal he sits behind a bullet-proof screen.
They have confiscated his uniform.
A cardie and open-necked shirt do not constitute
the image he would like to project.
The steel-grey mortuary hair, a gift to cartoonists,
has a straggly look, as though his enemies
have tousled him for the cameras. So, when he refuses
to recognise the court and hammers a shoe
on the desk between him and his judges,
he is done for already, takes on the impotent look
of a small, fat man in a temper –
the kind who would sign orders and feel no need
to think of the victims or picture their faces.
The evidence approaches like a wrecking-ball
that will sweep him away, though somewhere behind
that bullish face, those bullet eyes, he has not yet lost
the will to out-rant his accusers, the conviction that he will win.

The Interpreter (1)

In a packed train from the suburbs I revise
irregular verbs and acquaint myself
with the extensive vocabulary of atrocity.
I am fluent enough to know that nobody is fluent,
even in his own language. Always suspect a nuance.
What is being said in the underground tunnels
of the unsaid? How does an arrangement of the face
or a change of timbre affect what is stated?

From photographs used in evidence and sudden
bright doors opening in the testimony,
I begin to picture a village in remotest Europe,
unlucky in where it lies, a dozen miles
from the disputed border and at the mercy of both sides.

There are modest statues in the village square
to the dead of two world wars and, now, the memorial
for which the place is known – the victims' names
chipped on a marble wall next to the space
I translate as 'Playground of the Fatherless'.
I learn of the region's rich woodland,
the lakes of bluebells and the part they have played
for centuries in the villagers' lives. A band from a neighbouring town
turned out to play when the main street to the woods
was re-christened '10 April Street'. You would scarcely believe
how much I know about the village dogs,
both those that fled the soldiers' arrival
and those that died, baring their teeth at the guns.

Witness A

The cameras have made her the world's mother
and she knows it, wearing a different outfit
every day, her local idiom a permanent challenge
to the interpreters. She grumbles while the guards
straighten her cushions and help her adjust
the ear-phones, then settles to the gossip of her life.
The judges manage what they seem to consider
neutral smiles and indulge her performance.

She was forty the month the massacre took place.
She had gone alone for a walk in the woods, an hour or so
of rambling that took her miles from the village.
It was a habit of hers. She loved the fresh leaves and bluebell lakes.
A quiet snigger in the gallery, a disbelieving grunt.
When she heard the shooting she turned and ran for home,
fearful for her husband and two children
and the lives also of her parents. The closer
she drew to the shots and screams, the more she knew
she had to stay hidden. That was how she witnessed
the 'mass murder', as she called it, run its course.
Over two hundred villagers, among them women and children,
machine-gunned to death at the edge
of a shallow pit clearly intended
to be their communal grave. After a while
she crept away, but not before she had had a close look
at the officer-in-charge of the killing.

The Accused was there. She had definitely seen the Accused
directing the machine-gunners. The Accused, ten yards away,
taps his head, as much as to say
'crazy woman'. She staggers to her feet,
ugly with intent and has to be restrained,
her scarf awry and tears running down her face.

'I saw you there.' The recording equipment
has somehow wrapped itself around her.
All the while, the interpreters joke about the translation
of swear words and, hands over microphones,
enjoy an exchange of not-so-scholarly smut.

The court adjourns
for half an hour, the judges unaware
of the kerfuffle outside the door, a vicious face-to-face
between the witness and a woman her own age:
'You lying bitch. You were nowhere near
the killings. You were meeting my husband
in the woods and not for the first time. Not enough
that you slept with married men, now you must also be
the heroine and survivor.' Each in a pool
of her supporters, the women are whirled
down the magnificent stone steps, hustled
away in different directions.

Witness B

They called her the Lazarine. She wore
the necklace of death and set her face to the world
in ways beyond tears and laughter.
The others kept their distance, wary of one
who had lived twice and now, for the second time,
told how the soldiers' final act
was to step into the pit and cut the throats
of those who were still moving.
How she rolled, face-down, into a pocket of still air
between two corpses and lost consciousness.
She had no memory of the earth covering her
but carried with her the face of the Accused
as the officer-in-charge. Now chanting
her ordeal, she stopped, opened her blouse
and, to gasps from the courtroom, bared the scar on her throat.
She dreams of a country of grief, she says, under
a forest of willows, but the judges,
embarrassed, decline to hear it described.
No matter. It was as if the dead
themselves had returned to bear witness
and had the last word and were not to be doubted.
Later, in the park, she stood under the trees,
her upturned face dizzy with birdsong –
the same sound that had pierced her as she slipped towards death,
then sweetened her crawl back from oblivion,
trailing blood and earth.

The Accused (2)

There are few males in the courtroom,
but when the judges enter the women stand in unison, raise
the framed photographs of their husbands and sons
and cry for justice. And again when the Accused
is led in – they cry now for justice and revenge.
The Accused exudes indifference and shades of contempt.
Once, with an amused look,
he aims his finger at the gallery and feigns pulling a trigger.
The courtroom has to be cleared.
He is rumoured to be 'on twenty-four-hour watch',
to have 'got religion', or at least, acquired a crucifix.
Now, as the evidence against grows like a mountain,
he is given to maniacal, high-pitched laughter,
either mocking the widows, or having a breakdown,
or embarking on the behaviour patterns
that will have him declared 'unfit for trial'.

The Interpreter (2)

So far as I can tell, some of them are lying,
or at least failing to tell the exact truth,
if that exists. They offer versions coloured
by themselves and the years between,
folkloric flourishes, small embellishments,
the distortions of faulty memory.
The truth will never be unthreaded fully,
though enough, perhaps, will be accepted
to secure the Accused
his date with the hangman.

Next week the Defence will do what it can
to discredit this week's witnesses. The Accused
will brand them all a shower of traitors.
There will be a full house for the undertaker's son.
The widows will turn their backs on him
in murderous silence, cursing his seed and breed.
The concepts of provocation and self-defence
will have their shameful outings
and the Accused's writings will be used selectively
to portray him as, at heart, a patriot. Someone is sure to say
that History is both our guilt and our stab at redemption.
Redemption, if the trial goes that far, will begin
at dawn, in a prison yard, on the end of a rope,
and at dawn the same day in a village square that streams
with 'Welcome Home' banners and bunting,
hanging baskets and international peace flags.
Bells will tumble in the tower with an Old World fervour,
as though innocence might again be possible.

Witness G

The undertaker's son has spent three years
in solitary for his own protection.
After threats to his wife and children – or so he claimed –
it was he who buried guns and explosives in the woods,
the Accused's justification for attacking the village.
A star witness now for the Prosecution
and quick to denounce the Accused, he has not,
however, been, and never will be, forgiven.
On the day of the massacre he drove his wife and children
to visit relatives in another village.
No one with family dead can ignore
such ruthless self-interest, or accept his failure to warn.
So he runs the gauntlet of kindly women's curses.
His family has moved away, his house is aerosoled
with threats and condemnations.
He will change his name and grow anonymous
among the terraces of a distant city.
He will be tracked down before the year is out
by his third cousins and left dead in the snow.

The Interpreter (3)

God forbid I grow old as a connoisseur
of Man's depravity. After days like these –
stained with hatred and the cut-throat past –
in search of the benign I choose to walk
home through the park.
I would, if I could, compose an interpreter's prayer –
names in a clean recital, pitched to move
whatever good may bask at the heart of things.
'Squirrel,' I think, 'a small arborean rodent';
'bluebell: an Old World plant of the lily family,
with blue, bell-shaped flowers'.
I think 'leaf' and 'light' and 'water'.
I think 'street' and 'sky'.
Not much there, you might say, to counter the thrust
of a pitiless, cut-throat future –
yet it counts that the urge is alive,
that somehow the field has not been abandoned.
I think 'grass' and 'rabbits' and 'hostels' and 'hot dogs'.
I think 'houses' and 'stone'.
Let the final word be 'darkness' as darkness comes down.

Witness J

The teenager, alive because he played truant
on the fatal day and has ground to make up,
breaks a leg kicking the prison van
in which the Accused arrives at the courthouse.
He delivers what evidence he has from a wheelchair.
His father and his teacher are not around
to administer the sharp rebuke.

The Interpreter (4)

I think of the places where the truth was lost:
in the corner of a bar where six men met –
or was it five? No record of what was said
or who said what or what was decided.
Twelve people lost their lives in the feud
that followed. Claims and counterclaims.
What of the rumours of collusion, those darkened cars
parked in the woods, as for a lovers' tryst.
Denials on all sides, bullets in the post,
and several public figures fleeing abroad.
Not one page of their ghost-written memoirs can be trusted.
And who shot the Minister of Defence in that famous square
in the capital where the nation lives its history?
Was it a rebel conspiracy, or army factions, intent,
if others are to be believed, on provoking civil war?
At café tables, on trains and buses, wherever
two or three were gathered, the truth was lost.
In kitchens too, in hospital corridors, in the chambers
of august institutions, the truth was, at best, approximate
or carefully re-aligned.
As one Professor of Politics dared to remark,
'We're all revisionists now and shall be again.'
Meanwhile, our three judges stoutly pursue
the evidence there is to be had from the witnesses' memories.
Whatever emerges will be labelled Truth.
The Accused will hang or be confined
to a psychiatric hospital, the party in power
will begin to re-write the text books. The past will feed
its truth into the present, the present process the past
as year after year the bones of the Disappeared rise
from bogs and forests and deserted beaches,
bringing one kind of truth, the truth of the mortuary slab,
and year after year the testimony of those who stayed silent
may open paths to where the truth was lost.

The Undertaker's Wife

My husband knew more about death than anyone else
in the village, dressed to encounter it daily
in the living quarters above the 'shop' –
a word he hated, preferring instead to speak
of the 'business', those two rooms on the ground floor
that were never without coffins, empty or full.
Nobody else in the village had handled the dead
as he had, laid out the elders for the grave
in their final nakedness. These family intimacies
coloured his rapport with the villagers headstone grey,
made his smile a sliver of frost, his eyes
the dark archive of a man who could write
a history of death. I married him as my last chance
and was not offended when my friends
joked about 'cold hands', or were curious about the skills
he brought to our bedroom. I countered
with the traditional claims for a 'warm heart'.
The boy we adopted was from a village
beyond the mountains. It was the time
when unidentified groups came out of the woods
and took prisoners, nobody knew where or why.
When he was six, they chose his parents
while he hid in the woodshed. He never saw them again
and came into our lives so fraught and anxious
we thought he would run away. But year by year
he took his place among the villagers
as the undertaker's son, a man of consequence,
accepted by them and taught to smile
by the village girl he married, and unpicked
from the black fabric of his past
by his own children. But to him
the past did not recede or slacken its grip.
Something or someone had him by the throat.
The less we knew the better, or so it seemed.

The day before the massacre he packed us off
to live with relatives. Our lives changed overnight.
The survivors were implacable. If he knew
enough to save his family, he knew enough
to warn the entire village. His failure to warn
meant a hand in every death.

They left him dead in the snow
in a foreign city. We made the journey
to bury him and claim his family.
We live here still among the grudging faces
among the vengeful who would do us harm
when the cameras go and we are half-forgotten.
Outside the homecoming night is ablaze
with fireworks. Our cases packed, we lie
under a thick coverlet and think of the future,
eyes open, staring into the dark.

The Accused (3)

The existing photographs, in retrospect,
seem to record an unsmiling intent,
that angel-of-death stoniness against a blurred background,
suggesting a shadowy past. The Defence argues
that he too is a victim.
The evidence they cite is not widely known:
the slum poverty of his boyhood,
his father's brutish presence, bequeathing hatred
and more hatred, the death of his mother
when he was five. They try to disperse the fog
of rumour – that he led a murder squad
during the War of Liberation,
that he became, for a time, a police informer,
that he smuggled guns from Africa,
was on first-names terms with half the world's tyrants.
All myth, all speculation, unprovable, the Defence avers.
The Accused stares in silence into his hands.
For several days becomes a fugitive half-hidden behind
what may be a false name, among dates and events
that are plainly inaccurate.
Is the wrong man on trial? From the widows' faltering need
for reassurance, reassurance grows.
Day in, day out, their fixed, implacable eyes
begin to fathom his fear.

The Interpreter (5)

On days when the Court adjourned early,
the women gathered in the spacious lobby
of their all-expenses-paid Government hotel.
They loved the revolving door and the endless surprise
of seeing themselves reflected four times simultaneously
in the lobby mirrors. There were three widows
who went for walks together, even when fog
was a grey phlegm in the park, the river invisible
and the massive bridges weighted with shadow.
I knew their faces from the Courtroom, they mine
and they accepted me, at a distance.
You'd think they might visit the department stores,
or splash out in a modest way on a novelty item,
or be photographed with an assistant.
But no, they took their widowhood seriously.
Call me fantasist, but today
as I watched them emerge from the fog,
a little less stiff, a little less severe, like sadness thawing,
I savoured their formal greeting. Soon they will smile
and whatever a smile may recover will slip
back into their lives. And whatever darkness
they thought might be their portion
will give way to light on their faces,
tough and crepuscular and stronger than anyone knew.

The Willow Forest

What with the pogroms, the genocide,
the ethnic cleansing, the secret massacres,
the mass graves, the death camps, the public executions,
at last there was nobody left,
the country was empty.
Survivors who reached the borders
became refugees.

Rebuked by that silence beyond the mountains,
the victors planted willows and in due course
the country grew into a willow forest.
The trees hung their heads
over a history that, now memorialised,
could be forgotten.

Except that the few who visited
spoke of a weight
that was more than gravity,
a wind in the trees
that stilled to a kind of weeping.

NOTES

The National Anthem
The first stanza is a phonetic nonsense version of the opening lines of 'The Soldiers' Song', national anthem of the Republic of Ireland. 'Fuck-all' is a play on 'focal', the Irish word for 'word'.

Twenty-six Irish Paintings
I am indebted to Julian Campbell for his catalogue, *The Irish Impressionists: Irish Artists in France and Belgium 1850–1914* (The National Gallery of Ireland), in which I found the paintings which prompted this set of poems.

Side Effects (2)
Sweeney is a character from Irish mythology. As a result of a cleric's curse, he is driven mad by the din at the Battle of Moira and spends years in the wilderness, often naked and living in trees. Throughout this period, he composes nature poems.